AUTOBIOGRAPHY

A FRIEND IN THE LIBRARY

A Practical Guide to the Writings of

RALPH WALDO EMERSON

NATHANIEL HAWTHORNE

HENRY WADSWORTH LONGFELLOW

JAMES RUSSELL LOWELL

JOHN GREENLEAF WHITTIER

OLIVER WENDELL HOLMES

IN TWELVE VOLUMES

VOLUME XII

A FRIEND IN THE LIBRARY

AUTOBIOGRAPHY

BY

EVA MARCH TAPPAN

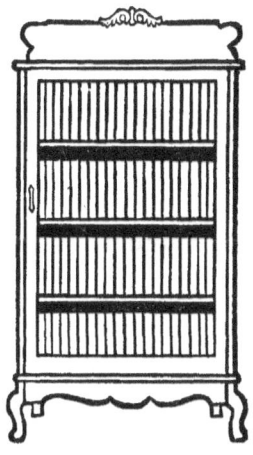

British Library Cataloguing-in-Publication Data
A catalogue record for this book is available from the
British Library

Eva March Tappan

Eva March Tappan was born on 26th December 1854 in Blackstone, Massachusetts, America. She is well known as a factual as well as fictional writer, but spent her early career as a teacher. Tappan was the only child of Reverend Edmund March Tappan and Lucretia Logée, and received her education at the esteemed Vassar College. This was a private coeducational liberal arts college, in the town of Poughkeepsie, New York, from which she graduated in 1875. Here, Tappan was a member of Phi Beta Kappa, the oldest honour society for the liberal arts and sciences, widely considered as the nations most prestigious society. She also edited the *Vassar Miscellany,* a college publication.

After leaving her early education, Tappan began teaching at Wheaton College, one of the oldest institutions of higher education for women in the United States, founded in 1834 and based in Norton, Massachusetts. She taught Latin and German here, from 1875 until 1880, before moving on to the Raymond Academy in Camden, New Jersey where she was associate Principal until 1894. Tappan also received a graduate degree in English Literature from the University of Pennsylvania. This allowed her to pursue her first love, that of reading and writing, and she taught as head of the English department at the English High School at Worcester, Massachusetts.

It was only after this date that Tappan began her literary career, writing about famous characters in history, often aimed at educating children in important historical themes and epochs. Some of her better known works include, *In the Days of William the Conqueror* (1901) and *In the Days of Queen Elizabeth* (1902), *The Out-of-Door Book* (1907), *When Knights Were Bold* (1911) and *The Little Book of the Flag* (1917). Tappan never married, being a happy singleton, and died on 29th January 1930, aged seventy-five.

AUTOBIOGRAPHY

IT is always interesting to know about the
people who have "done things." If a man has
made a fortune, we like to hear how he made
his "first hundred dollars," how his property
increased, and what his business methods
were. If he has invented something, we cannot help feeling curiosity to know what first
suggested it to him, and whether he had a
hard time working out his thought, getting the
article manufactured, and arousing a demand
for it. If a man has painted pictures, we like
to learn whether he had help and encourage-
ment, or whether he had to meet opposition
and make his way among disadvantages. If
a man has written good books, we are always
glad if some one searches through old manu-

scripts and yellowed newspapers and discovers some of his early or forgotten writings. The lives of most of the celebrated people have been written, and these books are generally worth reading. One thing, however, would be still better, and that would be an autobiography of each one. Unluckily, people who are really doing anything are usually too busy to write autobiographies, and the custom of keeping journals has gone out of fashion. We may think ourselves all the more fortunate, then, if any one in whom we are interested has left note-books or diaries. We are especially favored in the case of Hawthorne, for his "American Note-Books" (xviii.), "Notes of Travel" (xix., xx., xxi., xxii.), and "Our Old Home" (xi.) give a vivid picture of his life and thought. They were edited by Mrs. Hawthorne. She enriched them by adding an occasional extract from a letter, and she made no omissions except of paragraphs that were of too personal a nature to be given to the public, and of some parts that had been published by him in other forms.

To turn the pages of these note-books is more than glancing at an outline sketch of Hawthorne's life; it is gazing straight into his mind and following him from day to day. He takes long walks into the country and by the sea (xviii. 4, 118; ii. 300), and writes of these with all his charm of minute description. He sees everything: the apple trees, "with only here and there an apple on the boughs"; "heaps of dry leaves tossed together by the wind as if for a couch and lounging-place for the weary traveler, while the sun is warming it for him"; the schooner which has run up an inlet of the sea and now appears "amid the rural landscape" (xviii. 113, 114). He notes that the little barefoot boy running up the path shows the soles of his bare feet (xviii. 84). He notes, what perhaps no one else has put into words, that on the beach "a dry spot flashes around your step, and grows moist as you lift your foot again" (xviii. 116). He sets down stray bits of knowledge which perhaps he fancies may be of use to him: what sort of hole is dug by an exploding shell, and that the windows of an old castle in England were made of beryl (xviii. 24). Nothing that is amusing escapes his eye. He writes of a certain "little mischief of a brunette," whose "manner of walking is by jerks, with a quiver, as if she were made of calves'-feet jelly"

4

(xviii. 87). He tells the story of "a fellow without money," but with plenty of mother-wit, who, "having one hundred and seventy miles to go, fastened a chain and padlock to his legs, and lay down in a field. He was apprehended and carried gratis to a jail in the town whither he desired to go" (xviii. 17).

The "American Note-Books" tell us bits of Hawthorne's life in Salem and at Brook Farm. He writes (xviii. 286) of Miss Margaret Fuller's "transcendental heifer" who was "apt to kick over the milk-pail," and of the author himself working with such "righteous vehemence" as to break the hay-cutter in ten minutes. He hopes that some day his books will enable him to buy or rent a little cottage. Before long it comes to pass that he and his wife take possession of the "Old Manse" in

Concord. Never was there a happier home, even though the river is slow, the rain sometimes falls, there is more fruit than they know how to dispose of, and the big black dog that peers down the avenue is too timid to come at the whistle of the master of the house. "Foolish dog," says Hawthorne, "if he had more faith, he should have bones enough." Emerson " drops in " frequently; Thoreau comes to dinner, and the first melon from the garden is cut.

Hawthorne writes of going to the Boston Athenæum (xviii. 470) and seeing Mr. Hildreth at work on his history of the United States. "It is very curious," he says, "thus to have a glimpse of a book in process of creation under one's eye." This is exactly the fascination that the "Note-Books" have for one who loves Hawthorne's work, for in them were written the thoughts and fancies from which many of his stories grew. In western Massachusetts he visited a lime-kiln and wrote a minute description (xviii. 235) of it, which he afterwards used in his "Ethan Brand" (iii. 112). His parable of "The Great Stone Face" (iii. 29) had its origin in a few lines in the "American Note-Books" (xviii. 252). He jots down the thought (xviii. 18), "To make one's own reflection in a mirror the subject of a story." Some time afterwards he wrote the story that this suggested, "Monsieur du Miroir" (iv. 220), the tale of the annoying gentleman of the looking glass who persisted in wearing waistcoats and cravats of exactly the same pattern as the romancer's; who moved his lips, but spoke never a word. This Monsieur plays many childish tricks. In a hardware store he is more than likely to stick his head into a new brass kettle, and sometimes he peers up from the very bottom of a well. "Were I to reach the sources of the Nile," declares Hawthorne, "I should expect to meet him there." The thought of absolute perfection interested Hawthorne. He writes (xviii. 119): "A person to be in the possession of something as perfect as mortal man has a right to demand; he tries to make it better, and ruins it entirely." Later, he is haunted by the same idea, and writes, "A person to be the death of his beloved in trying to raise her to more than mortal perfection; yet this should be a comfort to him for having aimed so highly and holily." Six years after the thought occurred to him, "The Birthmark"

(iv. 48) appeared, the story of the alchemist Aylmer and his beautiful wife, who is even dearer to him than his laboratory and his mystical researches. The one flaw in his bliss is the birthmark of a tiny red hand on his wife's cheek. Save for this, her beauty is perfect, and Aylmer sets to work with the aid of all his knowledge to remove the mark. He succeeds, but in the ending of the story it is most interesting to see how the author works together both of the thoughts which suggested it, and which one he regards as the higher.

In 1853 Hawthorne was sent to Liverpool as United States consul. Save in his dreams and fancies, he had hardly been out of New England, and everything across the ocean was as new and fresh to him as to his children.

He writes in his note-book of the English fashion of training peach and pear trees flat against a wall (xix. 8); of the epitaph, "Here rests in *pease* a virtuous wife" (xix. 46); of the "ponderous and imposing look of an English legal document" (xix. 167); of the "judicial wig," which, he says, seems intended to keep the judge from hearing any of the evidence. "It is like the old idea of blindfolding the statue of Justice," he declares (xix. 123). He gave a poor child a bit of silver and wished afterwards that he had given her ten shillings "and denied it to a begging subscriptionist," who had just fleeced him of that amount (xx. 63). Hawthorne was always exceedingly kind to children. In "Our Old Home" (xi.), much of which was taken from his note-books, he describes a forlorn child in a workhouse, most revoltingly disfigured by disease, who mutely appealed to be taken up. He would not disappoint the loathsome little creature, but took it up — after a mental struggle — and caressed it tenderly (xi. 440).

Together with all the sight-seeing, there was the work of the consular office, helping Americans and so-called Americans out of their difficulties, giving money to one, going to the police court for another, grieving when — as often happens to people who are not geniuses — the wrong word slipped out, and he called a man to his face an " acrid" critic, when all he meant to say was "severe" or "fastidious" (xx. 92). Speech-making was Hawthorne's horror. "It is the most awful part of my official duty," he writes (xx. 161), "this necessity of making dinner speeches at the Mayor's and

other public or semi-public tables." At the
dinner which called forth this lament, he was
seated beside an American lady of whom he
wrote pathetically, "She did not pity me at
all." At another civic banquet (xi. 507), he
begged one of his friends, "by whatever he
deemed holiest," to give him a thought to
start with. Complimenting the Lord Mayor
was suggested for a beginning. Hawthorne
says, "Seizing this handful of straw with a
death-grip, and bidding my three friends bury
me honorably, I got upon my legs to save both
countries or perish in the attempt."

In these journals, written for his own eyes,
the great romancer is delightfully frank in
revealing his thoughts on the simplest sights.
He writes of the pleasant familiarity of the
little birds with the colossal statues (xxi. 203),

and of the pet cat that did not put on airs (xxii. 354). He is amused by the speech of the hungry little boy who gazed longingly at an enormous porphyry vase (xxi. 269) and "wished that he had it full of soup." He visits Sir Walter Scott's old home at Abbotsford, and writes (xxi. 6) : —

It is an odd truth, too, that a house is forever after spoiled and ruined as a home, by having been the abode of a great man. His spirit haunts it, as it were, with a malevolent effect, and takes hearth and hall away from the nominal possessors, giving the whole world the right to enter there because he had such intimate relations with all the world.

Holmes's "Our Hundred Days in Europe" (x.), although it was written to be published, is almost as frank as Hawthorne's "Note-Books." Holmes has a fashion of telling

13

about himself and his own works that in almost any one else would be egotistical and conceited. In him, however, it is united with so delightfully childlike a confidence in our interest, — because he likes us and we like him, — that it seems only to bring us nearer to his kindly thought.

His "Our Hundred Days in Europe" (x.) was really a "fifty years after" visit, for his first trip across the ocean was made half a century earlier. He tells us in most familiar fashion how he happened to go, how kind people in England were to him, the complimentary verses that were written about him, and his "formal sentence as Doctor of Letters." He quotes the Latin speech made on the occasion of conferring the degree (x. 76), with its praise of "The Last Leaf" and the

Breakfast Table series, and says delightfully that he "would not do it for the world if it were not disguised by being hidden in the mask of a dead language." He travels with his daughter over a road running so close to the edge of a steep hillside (x. 102) "that there were times when every one of our forty digits curled up like a bird's claw." The book was written, as he says, "more especially for readers who have a personal interest in the writer"; but the friends of Holmes are so many that it might well have been dedicated to all who enjoy wit and wisdom, humor and kindness.

It is said that some folk can never write a letter without mounting a pedestal whenever they take their pens in hand; but I fancy that authors are rarely open to that charge. Maybe they become tired of remembering that their fountain pens have type-metal attachments, and that any *lapsus pennae* will be horribly repeated in at least every copy of the first edition, and is almost sure to be gathered up by critics of the carpet-sweeper variety. Be that as it may, some of the easiest, most natural, and most off-hand epistles in existence have been scribbled by famous authors to their friends, without an apparent thought of the volumes of "life and letters" that are so sure to follow any literary success.

Of all the collections of these familiar letters that have been made, there are none more charming than Lowell's, none that harmonize more perfectly with the man in his books, or that help more to strengthen and make clear the ideal of the poet himself in our minds. They begin with one written at the mature age of eight (xiv. 8), when he went to a party and reported that he "danced a great deal and was very happy." But "No one is always happy," as the ancients used to say, and the next following letter was written on a day when a twofold affliction had pounced upon him, and he had "the ague together with a gumbile." His taste for fine copies of books was not slow in developing, and when he was seventeen, he wrote a college friend of his delight in owning a "beautiful edition of Milton," and his determination "to read all the Greek and Latin classics," which he did. He writes a poem to "Our Old Horse-Chestnut Tree," he reads twenty pages in Cicero and eight chapters in Herodotus, — "all this of my own accord," he says.

Verily, "the thoughts of youth are long, long thoughts," for this young man of eighteen has decided to study law, and probably become Chief Justice of the United States, he declares. He thinks seriously of entering the Divinity School, but begins to read Blackstone; he thinks of studying medicine, then of finding a place in a store; but he hears Webster, and determines to go on with his law studies. When he has reached the wisdom of twenty years, he wonders (xiv. 44) whether there would be any opportunity for him to lecture in Andover. "They gave me four dollars in Concord," he writes; and adds, "I wish they'd take it into their heads to ask me at Cambridge, where they pay fifteen dollars, or in Lowell, where they pay twenty-five dollars!!"

AUTOBIOGRAPHY

All this time the real bent of his mind is toward literature. He writes poetry, and tries to behave so coolly about one of his poems in the "Knickerbocker" (xiv. 46) that his elder brother will not guess its author. Among his poems three or four lines long is, —

> Error is not forever; hope for right.
> Darkness is not the opposite of light,
> But only absence — day will follow night.

This was in 1839, when the unwilling law-student was wondering (xiv. 51) whether he "was made for anything in particular but to loiter through life." Five years later he gave to somewhat the same thought as that of the crude little poem its noble expression in "The Present Crisis" (i. 185): —

> Though the cause of Evil prosper, yet 't is Truth alone is strong,

And, albeit she wander outcast now, I see around her
    throng
Troops of beautiful, tall angels, to enshield her from
    all wrong.

Lowell was growing rapidly, and if he could have looked a few years ahead, he need have felt no anxiety about his intellectual progress at least. He was troubled about financial matters, and every word of appreciation of his poems was a double pleasure to him, because, as he wrote (xiv. 87), "it seems to increase my hope of being able one day to support myself by my pen." He had married Miss Maria White, who was "half of earth and *more* than half of heaven!" he said, and his affairs brightened, even financially, though the income that he names (xiv. 124) seems decidedly slender. He was delighted to receive thirty dollars for a poem. Forty-four years later the "New York Ledger" sent him a check for one thousand dollars (xvi. 251) for whatever he might choose to send.

Those days, however, were in the future, and there were many struggles to come before they could be reached, — and many letters to be written. One of these was to Longfellow (xiv. 137) and says of his "Rain in Summer" (i. 227), "Your poem, by the way, was published here at a very lucky season — just on the heels of a magnificent rain. . . . I am glad you had a kind word for the dear, patient oxen." Another letter is about his baby daughter, "Miss Blanche Lowell" (xiv. 154). One year later, he wrote "The Changeling" (ix. 251), for the dearly beloved little daughter had died.

A FRIEND IN THE LIBRARY

Lowell was deeply interested in the anti-slavery cause, and did much writing in its behalf. In debt as he was, he hated to take money for his anti-slavery work (xiv. 172). He wanted to go to New York, but "I cannot come without any money, and leave my wife with 62½ cents, such being the budget brought in by my secretary of the treasury this week," he wrote (xiv. 187). This is not a pleasant condition of affairs, but he draws amusement even from his annoyances. He says (xiv. 202), "I have not brass enough to be rich. A consciousness of external superiority to other men is painful to me. I never could ride in a two-horse coach with any comfort, I am afraid to meet the eyes of passers-by."

In 1853 the death of Mrs. Lowell overwhelmed him with grief. He wrote to a dear friend (xiv. 273), "She promised to be with me if that were possible, but it demands all the energy of the soul to believe without sight." An article which he had just written had won much praise, but he said sadly, "It came too late to please the only human being to please whom I greatly cared and whose satisfaction was to me prosperity and fame."

After Longfellow's retirement from Harvard, Lowell was chosen to take his place. He also became editor of the "Atlantic Monthly." His lectures to the students were real literature, but the amount of time demanded by the college work was a continual affliction to him. There is a wicked story that he once offered a student eighty per cent rather than read his essay! About this time he came into his inheritance, as he said, for the gout seized upon him.

It is just a little hard to be sorry for his aches
and pains when they resulted in so witty a
letter (xv. 22) as he wrote to his friend Miss
Norton. He makes a list of the advantages of
the disease. It provides an excuse for being
"testy," and in time he will be able to write
his name and keep his milk-score with his
knuckles, he declares; but he grieves that now
he must admit himself to be middle-aged, and
he fears that his verses "will no longer be ad-
mired by young ladies of sixteen." He wishes
some one would kindly tell him "what *has
happened* next week," to save him from the
"daily debauch of newspapers" (xv. 63). On
whatever subject he writes, he is always slip-
ping away into pure fun and frolic. Some of
the critics blamed him for using words that
drove them to their dictionaries, and in re-

sponse he sent a sonnet to the publisher Fields with some most delicious notes (xv. 192). "Glaucous" he defines as "between blue and green, an epithet of Poseidon, and an editor who shows greenness is sure to look blue in consequence." "Porkerlet" is "a pretty French diminutive, as in *roitelet*." He admits that he is becoming stouter (xv. 381), and says that his waist "has been growing more and more obscure (like many a passage in Browning) for several years." He declares that when he meets Emerson "the Fall of Adam seems a false report " (xv. 395).

Lowell had several times refused political honors, but in 1877 he accepted, though reluctantly, the appointment of minister to Spain. "I am 'H. E.' now," he writes (xvi. 14). "It is rather amusing, by the way, to see a certain added respect in the demeanor of my fellow-townsmen towards me, as if I had drawn a prize in the lottery and was somebody at last."

After three years in Spain, a cipher telegram was brought to Lowell. He was transferred to England. This was the greatest honor that could be paid to a diplomat, and Lowell wrote to his daughter (xvi. 75) that for the sake of his grandchildren, if nothing else, he should like to serve. That service was most acceptable to both countries, and full of honors; but he was glad to return to America. "If all go well, I shall see you again in June — one of the greatest favors I have to thank President Cleveland for," he wrote to Howells (xvi. 131) on his recall.

The letters of his last six years are far less overflowing with merriment than most of his earlier ones, but there is nothing dull about them. His thermometer is "a very serious one and not given to exaggeration" (xv. 199). He promises to write in his little English god-daughter's autograph album, "that she may have the pleasure of wondering one of these days how her mother ever could have loved so dull a fellow" (xvi. 200). He is thankful that "they can't landscape-garden the sea" (xvi. 238). He calls his gout "the unearned increment" from his grandfather's Madeira, and wishes "the cause instead of the effect" had been left him (xvi. 319). His man "continues to worry the lawn with his two machines, one of which perfects the roughness left by the other" (xvi. 321).

The last letter in the collection is a note to Leslie Stephen, written only a few weeks

before Lowell's death. The friendship between the two men was nearly thirty years
long, and the English author was asked to
write some reminiscences of him. He ended
his letter by saying (xvi. 325) : —

I have one strong impression which I can try
to put into words. It is not of his humor or his keen
literary sense, but of his unvarying sweetness and
simplicity. . . . There did not seem to be a drop
of bitterness in his composition . . . and I think
I may say that those to whom he is only known by
his books need not look far to discover that the
same Lowell is everywhere present in them.

AUTOBIOGRAPHY

ADDITIONAL

HAWTHORNE

The Custom House, vi. 1.
General Introduction, by Hawthorne's younger daughter, i. xi.
The Old Manse, iv. 1.

LONGFELLOW

Outre-Mer (vii.) is in great part Longfellow's letters to various friends written while he was abroad, and now cast into literary form. Of *Hyperion* (viii.) he says, "The feelings of the book are true; the events mostly fictitious."

HOLMES

Cinders from the Ashes, viii. 239.
The Autocrat of the Breakfast-Table, i. 209.
The School-Boy, xiii. 241.

All the poets have written poems marking events in their lives; for instance, Emerson's "Threnody" (ix. 148) was written on the death of his little son.

Whittier's "Snow-Bound" (iii. 134) pictures the poet's early home; "The Barefoot Boy" (ii. 126) describes his childhood; "Abram Morrison" (ii. 182) and "To My Old Schoolmaster" (iv. 73) are also reminiscences.

QUESTIONS

1. Why is there a call for biographies?

   Because we are interested in knowing about the people who have "done things."

2. Why are journals and note-books of value?

   Because they are generally written with frankness and simplicity.

3. Why are Hawthorne's note-books unusually valuable?

   Because they not only present a picture of the romancer's life and thought, but reveal the sources of many of his tales.

4. In his accounts of out-of-door rambles, what is especially marked?
The keenness with which he observes.

5. Name four of the stories, hints for which are given in his note-books.
"Ethan Brand" (iii. 112), *"The Great Stone Face"* (iii. 29), *"Monsieur du Miroir"* (iv. 220), *"The Birthmark"* (iv. 48).

6. What political position did Hawthorne hold?
Consul at Liverpool.

7. Why are his notes of his life in England so entertaining?
Because everything was new to him, and he wrote with freshness and genuine interest.

8. Why would Hawthorne have disliked to live in a house formerly owned by a famous man?

Because of his fancy that he would be only the nominal possessor; and that the intimate relations of the first owner with all the world had given all the right to enter.

9. Why is Holmes's custom of talking about himself not annoying?
   Because he gives us the feeling that he is treating us as intimate friends.

10. What was the groundwork of his "Our Hundred Days in Europe" (x.)?
    A visit to Europe which, at the age of seventy-seven, he made with his daughter.

11. How did it compare with his previous visit?
    At the first visit he was an unknown medical student; at the second, a world-famous author.

12. For whom does he say this book was written?

AUTOBIOGRAPHY

For readers who have a personal interest
in the author.

13. Who have written some of the easiest and
    most natural letters?
    Famous authors.

14. What permanent traits did Lowell manifest
    in his boyhood?
    Capacity for happiness, love of fine edi-
    tions of books, poetical fancy, and love
    of study.

15. Why did Lowell find it so difficult to choose
    a life-work?
    Because the whole bent of his mind was
    toward literature, and he was not at all
    sure that literature would support him.

16. What shows the growth of his mind between
    his twentieth and twenty-fifth year?
    His two expressions of the thought that
    evil is not permanent.

17. Why was he especially pleased at appreciation of his poems?

    Because it encouraged his hope of being able to support himself by his pen.

18. In what cause was Lowell deeply interested?

    The anti-slavery cause.

19. What literary positions did he hold?

    Professor at Harvard and editor of the "Atlantic Monthly."

20. By what qualities are his letters marked?

    Sincerity, affection, wit, and overflowing merriment.

21. What political positions did Lowell hold?

    United States minister to Spain, and also to England.

22. What strong impression did he make upon his old friend Leslie Stephen?

    An impression of sweetness and simplicity.